Parchment

A Prayer Quintet

Poems

by

John Tessitore

For Harry Partch
1901-1974

Cover Photo and Design by John Tessitore

Contents

Chromolodeon

From the Underground,
the sound of giant gears turning,
the dead saints dodging the cogs,
jealous of their peace in the catacombs,

too soon awakened from their slumbers
by the sound of the dynamo,
the antique machine of modern times,
another guzzler fueled
by the narrow escape,
powered by the hair's breadth,

demanding a living wage
as it dredges its own death.

It is unfashionable to prefer the sad eyes
of Chaplin to the stone face of Keaton
but I tramp again and want to hug my son
before I commit my acts of sabotage.

The spirit of my rebellion
must be…adolescent.
Its genius is lust,

to regain the wonder,
the excitement of lawless
chance, to feel the surge

and reject the enormous apparatus
of our freedoms—school boards
and senates, pundits and police forces—
to remember all the ways we trade
the simple for complication.

What did Székely say before his days on ice?

My kingdom!
My kingdom
for a slice
of bacon!

I am barely scraping by now.
I refuse to knuckle under.

I should have realized sooner
that power is, by definition, failure,

a fractured equilibrium,

like when I opened to the first page
of his scripture, written in living rage,
and the crazy old man told me
that we were all the same.

The Way of the rest of America
has always been to divide and conquer.

The good gray poet gave me something…other.

I've scribbled pages and pages of my own
since then but who am I to sing them?
Like the crazy old man, I am no one.
Amen.
Amen.

And yet…give me two pencils and my notebook.

I will drop them in my rucksack,
another Guthrie bindlestiff,
and head out
for the remaining territory.

Late. Always so late.

I wish I were younger, with fewer cares
and fewer responsibilities.

To do this now is insanity, I know,
a prayer for a prayer-less century (so far),
but is it crazier than relying
on the knowledge of history?
Is it crazier than denying all progress?
It it crazier than preferring the darkness of the past?
Is it crazier than rejecting the body in strict adherence to…
a someone
or a something?
Is anything as crazy as an eye in the sky?

Let me be capacious for once.
Let me sing the beautiful, lustful body.
Let me sing my dirty, filthy love.

But how to organize these fragments?
How to make sense of the composition?
How to replicate the orgasm?

What rational system
of communication
can help me explain
my dream?

grass trees tiles pebbles
wind rain water fire

Speaking about it will not hit the mark.

We can only have faith that the song
will not make the singer a liar.

Prophesy I

Chapter 1

the word is steadfast
our days are like the river
that hammers the gates of Nineveh
the word is solid as stone

the prophet is transition
the merchant the builder
the weaver who winds
the present together

with an agile sentence
he cries havoc sings a love song
curses his spite conquers night
the prophet is seldom wrong

the gift of sight
is given to poets
who ripen their words
in the warm earth of worship

holy holy sin and glory

Chapter 2

the prophet is not his story
not illness sorrow anxiety
not the sanctioned murder
not the severed finger
not the gruesome martyr
not the iron fetter
not the shrinking tumor
not the barren womb

the prophet is the word on paper
the poison we swallow together
the only sound in a quiet room

he speaks us into existence
the fragments discovered
in desert caves the dry bits
buried in broken jars
papyrus copper parchment

his word lasts longer
than the cities of the Lord
whose towers will fall
whose ruins will rise
the word is all that time
leaves behind

Chapter 3

a temple molders beneath the chapel
in catacombs the nests of asps
who slither to the henge
of a pagan slaughter
in the season of the flood
a drop of blood
seeps into the ground water

the word of the prophet lingers

Chapter 4

we speak together
through lines first written in April
during the second spring of plague

in the suburbs of New England
at the end of my early days

on paper I sing

it has been two weeks
since I lost everything

on paper I sing

many months since I
broke myself in two

on paper I sing

my love I sing
to you only you

holy holy sin and glory

Chapter 5

if our generation is doomed
to witness all of the endings at once
let us curse the moment of promise
let us curse the age of beauty

if time has stopped for all of us
it has reversed for me

naked did I arrive and naked will I return
a man of middle age sick and lonely
and yet I have no fear of death
and I deny its common sting
we are lovers of living or long to be

I feel your fingers on the paper
I grasp them as a lover
grasps the hand of a lover
I will hold you forever

this is the world we build together

Chapter 6

touch the ember to my lips
the coal we mine like magma
sere my soul in the faith of fire

let my word grow as grass
to cover my grave
let the seed stalk stand taller
than my tomb
let a dry wind scatter my ashes
the wind my pronouncement
let these lines be my monument

when my heart is empty
my right hand gathers

in scripture a bountiful harvest
in scripture perpetual spring
in scripture we are in season
in scripture a life everlasting

Chapter 7

from the sands we rise
to the sands we fall

the word is a rampart
a bastion a sanctuary
the word is a wall

they come for Masada under siege
they come for the son of Babylon
their legions like a river in flood
their footprints in blood
but the word endures the deluge
and the prophet sings of love

his song lasts longer than life
his song lasts longer than love

holy holy sin and glory

the prophet sings of love

New Harmonic Canon

Listen with me to
the woodblock melody,
the woodpecker rhythm,
the sapling strum.

In this forest,
a whole continent
manifests the music
of a dying season,
the gray sky gray stone
gray river basin,

adagio of the apple cart,
moonlight sonata of scraps.

We came. We saw.
We fell into the ocean.
Congratulations.

The best we ever were
or ever could be
was John Chapman
planting trees
and even he
was a goddamn
missionary.

I have to believe
that we will transcend
these stories, eventually,
that we will be free
of our history,
that even my dear mother
will not recognize me.

I am barely my reflection anyway.
Are you what you see?
Have you ever been that face
on the surface of the water?

Who am I to be ecstatic?
Who am I to compose a Mingus tune
on the back of an old psalm book?
The very idea fills the heavens with laughter.

Strike the cone gong again, my friend.

How is this even a poem?

[Insert here a Melville lesson on cetacean reproduction.]

In this frosty forest
on the far side of a century
I can only insist on my guilt
by association.

In this windowless cell
of a dimlit corner
of a moldy cellar,
I can only write my rebellion.

La Grande Ligne

I.

A pale sun rises and hides
behind a thin, white smoke
like a censer swinging over
dry pastures of asphodel.

Each year I mark the resurrection
with a poem that rings like a church bell.
Song of atonement. Psalm of welcome.

I yoke myself to grandfather's plow,
open the ground for the flower,
the tillers of wheat and lentil,
and sing an ancient prayer for water.

baavurah al timni mayim

We fade into gray anyway,
as the clouds twine together
to weave the cover of sky,
as a cold damp hangs in the air,
as a new blight threatens
the fields of barley and rye.

After a dark and broken winter,
our lives may be stunted forever.

II.

We try. *Elohai n'shama.* We try.

Our fingers are bitten by fire.
Our feet are broken on stone.

What more can we gather for gods
whose secret faces we've pressed
into seals of empire, whose armor
we've hammered from stolen ore,
whose splendor we've shined
to their shields until we saw
our meanness mirrored, our fate
in their slogans? (*Rape! Murder!*)

In our devotion we ignored
the cortege that followed them
in long procession. Furthest
was always best as we confessed
our sins, humbled ourselves
like servants, forever like children
before the promise of ankh and cross.

What more can we do to stanch
the bleeding, delay another loss?

III.

No honor remains
for the son
in sackcloth
who cedes himself
like property,
who suffers

for a subtle glory,
the red badge of tragedy.

Poor, innocent pilgrim,
that dream is empty.

IV.

Alone at night I sweat all hope
and enter. My mind has a mind
of its own, an instinct to spread
itself across the vacant space
like the branches of a tree.
My heart is hungry to sacrifice.
My mind resists humility.

Eli, Eli, lama sabachthani

IV.

I write my own story in verse
as an act of profane insistence.

My lines of ink like *kumadori*,
the greasepaint of the mime,
the long nose of Zanni.

I emulate every actor
who fills his mouth
with cotton, claims
the wisdom and candor
of a seer, a sybil
without a master,
a tongue of fire

set loose on the horizon,
a light that obscures itself.

I align myself with the singer
who sings like a lover.

V.

Sometimes I wonder if this is all,
this smallest gesture,
this modicum of character,
this angle that gives away
the entire architecture,
as if a man is a trick of selection,
a sifting of options
from a fragment of experience,
as if every seeker finds a cilice,
a silk cravat, a line of kohl,
a mislabeled relic.

How small a unit?
Which element?
What atom of integrity?

VI.

I worry that every pursuit
of my own person
repeats another theory,
as if I channel Epicurus,
explaining Democritus,
awaiting Lucretius.
A dust of random particles
to swerve a blank infinity.

Split the difference,
says Dogen Zenji,
Forget the self

or else, in your final moments
hone a pure true line of thought

but not some shoreline fragment
of *Shantih!* Surrender is too easy
if we can repair the narrative
with the solipsism of a writer,
the illusions of a deity.

VII.

And yet this is my greatest fear:
that we are just the talking cure,
the only order a poem that grows
by accretion. A nebula. A fusion.
The semen and ovum *resartus*.
I fear the us we are is just a process,
a figment our own description.

(Tell me, good Herr Doktor Breuer,
is the smallest unit the entire story?)

VIII.

I want to say something true,
discrete, as if I have an identity.
I want to renounce the vast lonely.
I want to redeem my dignity.

If there is anything left of me I give it
willingly. I cling my soul to your body.

IX.

baavurah al timni mayim

And in my dream I pluck
the earliest asphodel
whose roots once barred
the gates of Hell,
whose host once buried
the lost souls of Hades.

It is a sign, this flower
of mind that marks
the end of our days,
this dawning of another
silence. Its violent beauty
is our final prize.

I bless it in a drizzle
of rain, lay it at your feet,
and in my dream I sing
my lover's song:

I am the tare.
You are the wheat.

Mazda Marimba

A new fragility everywhere.

We are called to care for everything
lest we lose everything in despair.

I was raised for the gathering,
part magpie,
part salesman,
part film-flam,
a story-teller on the lam,

now a partisan of wreck and ruin.

The beast of the west
has broken almost…everything.

If it's too late for Rome,
we shall fiddle and sing.

I dreamed last night of Harry Partch
although I know so little about him,
only what I've gleaned second-hand
and after several hurried listens.

(I listen, but always hurried,
in my stride, like a blowhard.)

Scholarly genius of the junkyard,
tannery face and weathered hide,
sun-burned Steinbeck son-of-a-bitch,
way too comfortable among the bindles
and brutals east of Barstow…

to me he sounds like a hero.

What did it take for him
to look beyond The System?
What break? What pain?

What did he gain?
Was The Other Side his only prize?

I've spent too much time
trying to see myself
through different eyes,

gauging a glimmer
of recognition.

Perhaps I was primed
for his newfangled koto
by my recent "discovery"
of Lawrence Ferlinghetti,
Lorenzo Monsanto,

having already begun
my own flirtation
with compendium,

having written a poem
like a grab-bag mausoleum,
each line an inscription for my tomb,

having written,
in fact,
like him,

and others of course,
but feeling Coney Island
in my bones,

the illness of Brooklyn,
the smother of society,
all those crazy Sundays.

Is that something you can believe?
That I would absorb him first
and read him later?

Perhaps I was ready, finally.

Before a man faces his own trial,
every rupture seems mysterious.
Afterwards, fate feels like happenstance.

I survived
by never inspecting myself
too close…

until the blind prophet,
yours truly, collapsed.

Perhaps that's how Partch
found his bloboy,
his crychord,
his surrogate kithana.

(The words themselves
are worthy songs.)

Perhaps that's why
he took a hammer
to the cone gong
of an old, weird America.

Only now, in my forties,
have I learned to love
the Eyeball Kid,

the freakshow kink
Transcendental.

Only now in middle age,
do I tie an ugly bow
around a phase,

after failing to shed my clothes
for so long,

my aluminum siding,
my nylon curtain,

Tessitore the Teflon don.

Who could afford
to be the enemy
of such definition?

But here I stand
alone now, in my
liquid reflection.

Release me.
Release me.
Release me
into the great
and various world.

Our window
of opportunity
closes steadily.

John Tessitore has been a newspaper reporter, a magazine writer, and a biographer. He has taught British and American history and literature at colleges around Boston and has directed national policy studies on education, civil justice, and cultural policy. He now runs his own strategic communications business, First Idea Communications, and serves as Co-Editor Across the Pond for The Wee Sparrow Poetry Press. He has published poems in the *American Journal of Poetry*, *Canary*, *The Wallace Stevens Journal*, *The Ekphrastic Review*, *Gastropoda,* and *Wild Roof Journal*, and elsewhere, as well as three chapbooks: *I Sit At This Desk and Dream: Notes from a Sunday Morning on Instagram*, *We Are Becoming Unbound,* and, most recently, *All the Lonely American Roads.*

www.johntessitore.com
Twitter: @JohnTessitore2
Instagram: @jtessitorewriter
TikTok: @Jtessitorewriter

www.ingramcontent.com/pod-product-compliance
Lightning Source LLC
LaVergne TN
LVHW020543160826
845677LV00015B/4168
9798360000471